ENTP: 33 Secrets From The Life of an ENTP

By Diana Jackson

Contents

ENTP: Extraverted, Intuitive, Thinking, Perceiving

1. Seeks out ways to better understand their environment

Positive: ENTPs are always thinking and always analyzing, and though it might not sound like fun to everyone, just taking in an environment and figuring out how all the pieces fit together keeps them intellectually stimulated and entertained. While they aren't the most emotionally intelligent types, when it comes to a quick analysis of how to escape during a fire, the ENTP is top of the class.

Negative: All that ENTP talk, not a whole lot of ENTP action – that's the trademark of this type, an often-times brilliantly intellectual thinker and logician, who nonetheless doesn't do a whole lot with what they know – they're more prone to move on to some other problem that needs fixing, leaving someone else (a sensing type, most like) to handle the actual implementation of change.

In Relationships: It's a shame that ENTPs don't try to understand their mates as well as they do the electrical wiring in their home, because they have the potential for truly inspired emotional intelligence. For this reason, ENTPs would do well to find a less sensitive feeling type – someone who can stand up to them, while also teaching them how to consider others' feelings.

At Work: A hostile foreign situation – throw the ENTP in and this type could find out everything you need to know about what went wrong and how it has come to this. They are also one of the best personalities to figure out a way to bring the situation to a resolution. Just don't ask them to actually put their plan into action.

2. Quickly and accurately sizes up situations

Positive: The ENTP need only sweep his or her gaze around a party and they know, based on body language and body positioning around the room alone, who is having a good time and who is going to end up crying in a bathroom later. ENTPs have the capacity to take in a lot of information quickly, and they use it to avoid bad situations that they have no desire to be part of.

Negative: The thing about ENTPs is that, as outgoing extraverts, they have a tough time keeping their mouths shut, even when all the signs point toward the fact that they should. So they can come upon a situation, size it up in a matter of seconds or minutes, and then find themselves unable to stop from voicing their opinion as to how the matter should proceed – welcome or not.

In Relationships: If the ENTP is in hot water with his or her sweetie, they know it the moment they walk in the front door, though because this personality type is notoriously bad at handling people when they're upset, they might not be able to understand how or why with equal accuracy.

At Work: If ENTPs were more like their judging counterparts, they'd be born to take on leadership roles, but as it stands, these charismatic personalities would suit better in management consultation, where they come in, analyze a business or company, figure out how to make it run more efficiently and then move on.

3. Takes risks

Positive: The types of risks that ENTPs take are different than, say, that of an ESFP, who would be the first in line for skydiving. ENTPs instead take risks of the mind, daring to think what no one else will or could, and sometimes even saying the things that verge on outrageous or indecent. The world would be a boring place indeed without them.

Negative: Despite being grounded in reason by their thinking function, the ENTP's more audacious side comes out as a result of their willingness to take an argument and run with it, daring the other side to push the conversation into more and more outrageously impassioned territory. This can cause the ENTP to say something that they know might sting on a personal level – but they'll do it anyway.

In Relationships: ENTPs are quite open-minded when it comes to their relationships – if their significant other can best them in an argument, well, consider them smitten. But perhaps one of the more surprising aspects to the ENTP is how far they are willing to go in the name of love.

At Work: Perhaps the ENTP's love of risk-taking in both thought and word is most welcome at their place of work, and if they are given a great deal of latitude to innovate freely, their willingness to think outside of the box and go beyond what is known or accepted can be the harbinger for enormous change in our world.

4. Thinks very creatively

Positive: Perhaps the best thing about the ENTP's creative way of thinking is that, because they are also thinking types, their ideas stand a good likelihood of seeing the light of day. Because thinkers are logical and well-reasoned, the ENTP is most likely to stick with ideas that yes, push boundaries, but also make sense and could be turned into reality.

Negative: For all their creativity, ENTPs lack a more practical, day-to-day approach to life. While they might be at work, solving the problem of how the newest dinosaur bone discovery should be put together, the ENTP at home can have difficulty cooking chicken on the stove or might be a total loss when it comes to pressing his or her dress pants on the ironing board.

In Relationships: If they can focus their attention long enough, the ENTP is capable of some pretty thoughtful and creative surprises for his or her partner, and they're absolutely genius at pulling them off without a hitch, without their loved one so much as suspecting that something is afoot.

At Work: ENTPs are prized for their creative thinking abilities in the workplace, although their perceiving aspect can make it difficult to keep them pinned down and on-task. It will be the fight of the ENTP's life to see projects through from start to finish, but it's an endeavor they should embrace whole-heartedly, because there is so much they are capable of discovering.

5. Adventurous and outgoing

Positive: Unlike their introverted counterparts, who are more likely to stay home, musing to themselves for hours, extraverted ENTPs prefer to be among people they can chat and argue with (seriously, they love to spar!). Since they're more likely to be out socializing, ENTPs can end up in some pretty daring situations that push their physical limits – but the ENTP is more than up to the adventure.

Negative: The ENTP, like other intuitives who also have a perceiving function, utterly rejects the traditional, but with it can go their sense of boundaries. Adventurousness is a good thing, undoubtedly, but it must be tempered with sense and responsibility, or else the individual – like so many ENTPs – will go from flirting with the edge to toppling right over it.

In Relationships: ENTPs might not easily keep significant others (that pesky emotion part of relationship is challenging for them), but with their outgoing personalities and charming demeanors, ENTPs have no problem attracting romantic interests and keeping the atmosphere both fun and challenging.

At Work: ENTPs can easily be attached to jobs where they receive an assignment with a direct bit of description and then get sent out to accomplish whatever task requires their attention, even if that means traveling to the other side of the world. Not easily cowed by unfamiliar situations, the ENTP embraces adventure on the job.

6. Adaptable in changing environments

Positive: There's one in every group: that whiner who cannot handle it when their travel plans go awry or when Christmas plans change because someone got married. The great news? The ENTP is definitely not one of those types. Adaptable and open-minded, the ENTP simply absorbs the change and moves forward, no drama, no whining.

Negative: ENTPs aren't exactly chameleons, but they can have a somewhat maddening habit of switching positions on something, and they can do it when it's least welcome – like when you're at a party, you express an unpopular opinion, and you expect your ENTP friend to back you up – but they suddenly appear to be play for the other team.

In Relationships: If the ENTP has to move for his or her significant others, so be it; you won't see them pitching a huge fit over it. While they might regret leaving friends and even family behind, their sense of adventurousness keeps them flexible. Further, ENTPs are surprisingly adaptable when it comes to the life changes that accompany relationships – such as marriage, buying a house or kids.

At Work: One of the reasons ENTPs make such good consultants is because switching from location to location doesn't feel disruptive or disjointed to them; rather, they welcome the change of scenery and the opportunity to meet new people, to bring about some change, make some new connections or alliances, and then move on, switching gears as easily as a vehicle's automatic transmission.

7. Incredibly witty

Positive: The ENTP wit is razor sharp, the kind of cleverness that will leave people either breathless with laughter or stunned at the sheer virtuosity of the statement. As the veritable Oscar Wildes of their group of friends, the ENTP is much sought-after for his or her social and political commentary and critique.

Negative: Wit, combined with impulsivity (which is the next trait to be explored), can be a treacherous team, and the ENTP – whose thinking aspect leaves them particularly prone to insensitivity – can end up making that statement which is so biting and so harsh that the relationship with whomever they were speaking cannot ever be repaired.

In Relationships: If the ENTP's partner comes for the outgoing, gregarious personality, they stick around for the laughs, which pepper every situation and can be used to break the tension when tempers flare. ENTPs have a way of making even delays in the airport during the honeymoon a sophisticated laughing matter.

At Work: While introverts are just as capable of wit as the ENTP, this personality type is much more confident using their cleverness around people they don't know or have just met. This makes them excellent candidates for public service jobs or careers in the public sphere, where their obvious conversational intelligence will win over all those to whom they speak.

8. Impulsive, acts without thinking things through

Positive: Sometimes the ENTP just has an intuitive sense that a certain course of action is the right one, and they go for it. And whether or not it turns out all right (there's always that 50/50 chance), the real benefit is that the ENTP is courageous and unafraid to just try something new or different or bold.

Negative: The downside is that the ENTP's impulsivity can certainly backfire on them, causing a great deal of headache or a mess from which they must extricate themselves (or call on others to get them out of). Since ENTPs act impulsively as part of their nature, this perhaps happens to them more often than other, less perceiving types.

In Relationships: The ENTP can be either a hopeless romantic who does the crazy thing to win over their love interest; or, they might be the perpetual relationship failure, the person who does something without thinking and alienates their partner in the process, whether it's something as serious as cheating or a whole series of thoughtless smaller acts.

At Work: It's lucky that ENTPs have a talent for defending themselves, because with their impulsivity extending even to the workplace, they end up having some serious explaining to do. Sure, their spontaneous action might end spectacularly, but it is equally likely they'll end up making matters worse by arguing with their superior because they felt justified.

9. Personable and friendly

Positive: ENTPs have that air around them that says, "Hey you! Come say hi!" and they are equally as happy chatting up strangers in line at the grocery store as they are spending quality time with friends and family. They are just wonderfully personable and friendly people who welcome new acquaintances with spirit and enthusiasm, and they're happy to make others feel included.

Negative: Do you know why ENTPs so enthusiastically welcome new people into their circle? It's more of an invitation into the gladiatorial arena of verbal competition, because this personality type loves a good argument and wants to get as many points of view as possible – but they'll play devil's advocate and badger the poor, unsuspecting soul to tears.

In Relationships: One of the reasons ENTPs have such an easy time attracting potential romantic interests is because they present themselves to the world openly and honestly, with a confidence that's difficult to fake (though they can fake it if they have to). It's lucky they're so outgoing and willing to strike up a conversation with anyone, because they need sheer numbers on their side when it comes to finding someone who will stick around once the sparring starts.

At Work: While ENTPs prefer to work with a great degree of independence and flexibility, they still make for popular coworkers in an office setting. But, their outgoing personalities ensure that they make a positive impression when they interview for different positions, especially if they are given the opportunity to show off their incredible intelligence.

10. Interacts comfortably in large groups

Positive: Parties, crowds at the mall or exciting political rallies – the ENTP is at home anywhere where there are plenty of people for them to chat up. They thrive on the energy of a large group, and if they can make themselves the center of attention, hey – even better.

Negative: ENTPs can end up missing the boat when it comes to forging meaningful connections with people; they can end up with many acquaintances but few real, reliable friends. ENTPs should stop, think and focus occasionally on making more personal, one-on-one connections.

In Relationships: ENTPs can be the life of the party, so their partner had better either have the same energy or not mind being abandoned at pretty much every social function they attend together. The ENTP is going to hold back just because their spouse is shy (although it'd be surprising if they ended up with an introvert anyway).

At Work: Surprisingly, ENPTs could make great stand-up comedians, with their razor-sharp wit and their ability to play out the long-form joke. Best of all, they can face big crowds without a whole lot of stage fright, while comfortably playing to the company and making everyone laugh out loud.

11. At their best when they are the center of attention

Positive: ENTPs have so many superior qualities, they couldn't shrink like a violet if they wanted to, so it's a real advantage that this personality type is perfect at-home when lots of eyes are watching them (hostile or friendly; the ENTP isn't afraid to face detractors, and in fact takes great pleasure in shutting them down in front of everyone).

Negative: Divas. Attention-hungry. These are words that can describe ENTPs, and they are not nice descriptors. Can the ENTP get a little full of him/herself, basking in the attention and growing in arrogance? Well, they're human. With any luck, they have someone grounded to remind them of where they came from.

In Relationships: That person could very well be their significant other (if it's not some other family member), because they are more likely to listen to someone they view as their equal. The ENTP might not take a hint in the moment, but they can take a serious remonstrance from their sweetie afterward – or a whole series of them, after a whole lot of moments.

At Work: ENTPs are likely to receive some serious accolades throughout their career, and instead of being the awkward at the podium – you know, the guy or gal who is shuffling through their notes and coughing out their uncomfortableness – the ENTP will not only wing their acceptance speech, they'll have everyone rolling in the aisles. It's a tough job, but someone's got to do it.

12. Exceptional oral communication skills

Positive: Not only are ENTPs good at constructing a flawless argument on any topic or point of view, they can outline and defend it, out loud, with the fluidity and wit of any great Greek or Roman orator. Consider them the Michelangelos of the debate team in high school.

Negative: ENTPs like to hear themselves talk, and they assume that everyone else feels the same way, too. Unfortunately, this is not the case; while they are obviously gifted when it comes to making an oral presentation, once in a while they can forget that not all audiences are willing ones and end up making quite a spectacle of themselves.

In Relationships: On the plus side, ENTPs will communicate what they know, in the clearest possible terms, to the person they have chosen to share their lives with. Unfortunately, because they lack that intuitive emotional intelligence (not to be confused with their intuitive aspect), what they say might come out as insensitive.

At Work: As born talkers, who are not just good at it, they would willingly do it every day of their lives, ENTPs are in luck – there are plenty of careers that favor a fine, persuasive orator and will pay top dollar for the guy or gal who can win people over with their words. By working on their follow-through, ENTPs can become very successful TV personalities or actors.

13. Loves practical jokes

Positive: ENTPs are wonderful when it comes to practical jokes, because they will not only dish 'em out, they can take them graciously and with appreciation for the work involved. ENTPs would never turn up their noses at a situation where, even though they were the ones played for a fool, the pay-off was epic.

Negative: Like the things they say sometimes, ENTPs can get carried away with their practical jokes, not realizing that they have moved into offensive territory that could legitimately hurt someone's feelings. As far as they are concerned, it's all in good fun, but then they're not considering the POV of the person being pranked, who might have decidedly thinner skin.

In Relationships: Whether it's a quick scare when their spouse walks in the door or a more elaborate prank that took weeks to set up, the ENTP keeps his or her partner on their toes for the duration of the relationship, devoting to their practical jokes the kind of meticulous attention that, let's be honest, could be spent elsewhere.

At Work: Coworkers beware: the ENTP will work his or her way around the office, pranking each and every person without regard to age, gender or anything else for that matter. But, as mentioned, should everyone ban together and get them back for the years of torture and humiliation, the ENTP will show infinite appreciation where it is due.

14. Doesn't like to be coddled

Positive: ENTPs are almost boldly independent, and despite their love of company and attention, they don't want people fawning all over them or trying to take care of them. They take great pride in their ability to be self-sufficient, a trait that is most admirable considering how many people out there today are as helpless as children.

Negative: When the ENTP is sick, if you so much as try to press homemade chicken noodle soup on them, they might be dismissive and insist they are fine with canned. Come on, ENTPs – let people help you out a bit when you need it. They are stubborn and strong-willed, but no one can go through life completely unaided.

In Relationships: ENTPs don't just refuse coddling of their person, they aren't going to hand it out either, so their partners and families had better not expect a great deal of hand-holding. To be fair, though, the ENTP doesn't expect anything more for themselves, so they can hardly be labeled hypocrite.

At Work: Give the ENTP some clear, concise directions and then get out of their way, because they don't need anyone cheering for them and they would really prefer not to be micromanaged, with someone looking over their shoulder. While some bosses might think this is quite superb, others might be put off by the ENTP's rather combative attitude.

15. Concerned with theory, rather than practical application

Positive: There are plenty of people out there in the world who thrive on hands-on, practical problem-solving, but in many cases they wouldn't know where to start if it weren't for people like the ENTP, who dares to dream up the next big innovation, and does so in a manner that is attainable and realistic.

Negative: The problem with the ENTP's focus on the theoretical, rather than the practical, however, is that unless their ideas are picked up by someone – as in a work situation, for instance – the most incredible innovations can stay stuck inside the ENTP's mind and never see the light of day.

In Relationships: ENTPs dream of going on splendid, exotic vacations, but without the help of a more Sensing, practical partner the trip might not get off the ground. After all, someone has go to book the flight and hotel, pack and arrange to have the mail held at the post office. That person is definitely the ENTP's mate.

At Work: ENTPs make great scientists, as long as they're not the ones responsible for actually running the complex experiments in the laboratory. No, ENTPs are the ideas people who can puzzle over a problem, theorize a solution and then pass the baton to someone more comfortable with rigid protocol.

16. Loves a spirited argument

Positive: ENTPs could argue anything, anywhere, any time, and they would just as readily argue for something they don't believe in (just for kicks) as they would for a topic about which they feel passionately. It's not everyone's cup of tea, but it keeps the INTP sharp, giving them mental challenges to practice for when their arguing skills are truly needed.

Negative: Other types have a difficult time understanding what is so enjoyable about an argument – all it leads to, as far as most of the world is concerned, is hurt feelings, but the INTP doesn't have the capacity to stop, once engaged. Even if someone is clearly trying to pull out, the ENTP reaches out and says the thing that drags them back in.

In Relationships: If you want to be with an ENTP, you had better bring a whole wallop of patience and a few perfectly constructed arguments of your own. In fact, the ENTP who was on the fence about a new significant others will fall headlong in love the second he or she bests them in a battle of wits.

At Work: ENTPs use spirited arguments at work not as a means of dividing and conquering, but as a technique for brainstorming, to draw out the very best ideas from whatever is left after they and their coworkers have picked something apart from every angle. Many fields in the sciences only exist because people argued over all of the finer points.

17. Flexible and adaptable to change

Positive: If you want to change the time at which you meet your ENTP friend for lunch, no problem. If the dates for their big trip to Vegas must be moved around a bit, not an issue. ENTPs are flexible with their time and accepting of change, reasoning as they do that very little is worth getting worked up over.

Negative: Flexibility can become something like a habit, and while the ENTP presents a confident demeanor to the world, constantly going with the flow can make them something of a pushover. When it comes to the changing of an event or person that they truly care about, their habit for flexibility can lead them to some pretty hurt feelings.

In Relationships: ENTPs temper their argumentative personalities with a more relaxed lifestyle that is easy to be part of. Certainly in the early stages of a relationship the ENTP feels no need to put a label on anything, and he or she makes no excessive demands of time. This allows them to get to know people better at a slower, more relaxed pace, rather than jumping all in.

At Work: ENTPs are great for traveling jobs, especially ones where the destination changes frequently and suddenly. Because their personal lives tend to be less bolted down, they have the freedom and flexibility to switch things up from one week to the next, far more than a family man or woman who has kids and a spouse desiring their immediate attention.

18. Not easily offended

Positive: Even if you disagree whole-heartedly with what your ENTP friend is saying – heck, even if you personally attack them while in the midst of an argument, this personality type has skin thicker than a rhino's. Being that they themselves are prone to saying things that can come across as rude or insensitive, they won't hold it against anyone else.

Negative: The problem here, then, is that the ENTP believes as long as it's all in good fun, and as long as everyone knows the name of the game, each side has free rein to say what they will. But not everyone – not nearly everyone – has the emotional toughness of the ENTP, who can easily misinterpret someone else's intentions and go for the jugular.

In Relationships: ENTPs are challenging to share space with in the sense that their running commentary might drive you up a wall. Yet one of the best things about this type in a relationship – a cohabiting relationship at that – is that they have a much higher tolerance for the silly things that wear on couples who live together, and they won't take a wet towel lying on the floor as a personal affront.

At Work: Go ahead and give the ENTP your best critique in the workplace – they dare ya. Unlike more feeling and introverted personalities, this extraverted thinker is not just open to critique, they welcome it. Just don't get offended if they fire back with all the reasons their project is perfect (even if it isn't, they want to test you and see if you'll stand your ground).

19. Enjoys doing dangerous things

Positive: If something rests along the highway to the danger zone, you can bet the ENTP is zipping along that road in their flashiest sports car. ENTPs have a need for speed, among other things, like that feeling of sweat trickling down their brow as they climb a vertical rock wall in a national park on their day off. Dangerous activities like this are immensely appealing to ENTPs, keeping them fit and happy.

Negative: The sad fact is that the ENTPs are willing to do things that put their lives in danger (more than, say, your average Joe just going through life doing regular "dangerous" things, like flying in an airplane). Skydiving? Mountain scaling? Camping in the desert? Deep sea fishing? All extremely exciting, but all entirely dangerous activities that could end in untimely death.

In Relationships: Like a lot of other extraverted types, the ENTP might meet their potential best partner while partaking in the activities that get them out of the house and among the crowds. It's no surprise if the ENTP and his/her mate, when asked at a party how they met, reply, "Lion taming class at the circus."

At Work: ENTPs can take the types of jobs that the rest of us only see in movies. Don't doubt that your ENTP friend could be a spy for the CIA or lives an Indiana Jones-type existence that no one knows about. They'd do this dangerous stuff for fun, but it's even better that someone is willing to pay them for it.

20. Values knowledge

Positive: There's a movement in this world today, away from learning. Higher education and serious book reading might not be for everyone, but everyone can agree that when more people have a wider range of knowledge, the world is a better, more enlightened place. The ENTP does his or her part to shatter the status quo and inspire others to want to know more about the world.

Negative: Knowledge is certainly an important key to understanding, but so is experience. ENTPs, because they are ideas people and have a tendency to jump from project to project, can miss out on the experience of actually helping their great ideas come to physical fruition, which is itself an education and a lesson in patience, constancy and discipline.

In Relationships: ENTPs might not actively seek out intellectuals (they tend to keep their noses in books, rather than crave adventure) but they do want to be with people who value lifelong learning just as much as they do, so a couch potato who loves reality TV in their downtime will not suit for very long.

At Work: Even if ENTPs do have a tendency to jump from project to project, coming up with the big, brilliant ideas, they are nonetheless absorbing all the new information that they can for as long as they are working on something. They take this knowledge with them wherever they go, whether it's another project or job or even in their personal lives.

21. Dominant in interpersonal situations

Positive: ENTPs have a way of getting what they want, thanks to their powerful presences and their way of dominating a conversation. It's not that they don't listen to the other party – they are just as curious about what people have to say as they are excited to share what they think – but they will deftly steer conversations in the direction of their choosing.

Negative: A lot of people don't respond to this kind of manipulation positively, and they can view it as controlling or intimidating. Rather than rise to the challenge, many people who come into contact with the ENTP choose to just end the conversation as quickly as possible and make a mental note not to interact with that person again.

In Relationships: ENTPs might try to be dominant when it comes to their significant others – not in an abusive way, but in an "I like getting my way" kind of mindset – but they absolutely need an equally powerful partner who will call them on their greediness or selfishness and who will stand up to them and tell them "no" – tell them "no," and mean it, and not back down.

At Work: ENTPs, if not for their perceiving aspect, would dominate in the business and corporate world, but they're just not cut out for long-term, strings-attached, responsibility-laden careers. However, as business consultants they get the freedom and novelty of new projects and clients, plus the ability to teach others what they know about being the most impactful person in the room.

22. Exhibits careless behavior sometimes

Positive: While there is a difference between careless and carefree, the ENTP displays both, and they are often interchangeable for this most spontaneous of personality types. While careless people aren't often viewed with a positive lens, the ENTP displays an enviable insouciance that is at once cool and collected in most any situation.

Negative: If the ENTP exhibits careless behavior sometimes it must be said that it is motivated, at least in part, by the fact that they *are* rather careless when it comes to small details and minor, mundane tasks (and anything else that bores them). The unfortunate thing is that, when you are an adult, you don't get to choose everything you do and do not care about – you just have to suck it up and pay attention.

In Relationships: Perhaps the one person who feels the effects of the ENTP's carelessness the most is his or her partner, in all the little ways they forget to do things (or don't think to at all) in the home. ENTPs need a patient, guiding hand so that they can learn to be more thoughtful for others.

At Work: ENTPs just might forget an appointment or perform a task sloppily (if it's not in their wheelhouse of interests, it might as well have the agency of manure shoveling to them), but at the same time, their careless attitude can be a boon when they want to show a "poker face" to a client or rival, emoting total confidence.

23. Socially magnetic personality

Positive: ENTPs are the types of people who draw in other people by virtue of simply being themselves. They radiate confidence, assurance and charm, even if they're castigating someone while in the middle of a debate. Since they can always count on meeting new people wherever they go, the ENTP network is formidable.

Negative: The problem with always attracting people to you is that, sooner or later (probably sooner) you attract the wrong sorts. While the ENTP is more capable than other types to discern who is a toxic addition to their lives, they can have a more troubling time of getting rid of those people.

In Relationships: As mentioned, ENTPs have no trouble attracting people to their side, and they might find that they have a number of romantic interests to choose from at any one time. What matters is the part after they choose, however; ENTPs can find it difficult to hold onto someone who isn't wired the same way they are, and who might feel the sting of their wit before saying, "Buh-bye!"

At Work: ENTPs like to work with a great deal of autonomy and freedom, yet that doesn't mean that they prefer to work in isolation. Quite the opposite, in fact, as ENTPs are the types of people who work best when given an assignment or a mission that involves persuading or convincing people in their own way.

24. Tends to avoid organized religion

Positive: Religion is a magnificent comfort for some, but the ENTP's rejection of it does free their minds from some of the bigoted opinions that can arise from strict adherence to a set of beliefs laid down hundreds, if not thousands of years ago. This includes racism, sexism and homophobia, all of which are manifested today, by some, thanks to organized religion.

Negative: People without faith are very much in the minority, and can find themselves persecuted for their lack of belief and derided by people who cannot fathom a life lived without some sort of deity. ENTPs don't make the situation any easier for themselves, because they tend to be outspoken and argumentative, if only for the sake of a lively debate.

In Relationships: It can be very difficult for an ENTP to sustain a long-term relationship with someone who is religious – even the tiniest bit. There is definitely a spark in the ENTP that will quickly drain the religious partner on the topic of why they believe what they believe. The ENTP could never tire debating it, but their significant other certainly will after the fourth or fifth round.

At Work: As long as the ENTP isn't working for a church, their lack of belief should not be an issue. Perhaps if coworkers discover that they have no religious affiliation or faith (which they are bound to do, since ENTPs air their views without hesitation) opinions might change and arguments break out, but that's all to the good as far as ENTPs are concerned.

25. Has strong, clear communication skills

Positive: ENTPs refuse to beat around the bush when it comes to expressing what they want. Some people might be a bit astounded by their straightforward means of communication, but it is truly a refreshing change of pace in a world that is dominated by mealy-mouthed cowards who can't be upfront with themselves and others.

Negative: ENTPs can absolutely put people off with their straightforward way of speaking their mind. Their thinking function, combined with this personality type's extraversion, means that they don't have much by way of an inner censor, so no matter what type of company they're a part of, they feel perfectly comfortable saying the blunt, even rude thing.

In Relationships: ENTPs will be the first to admit that they don't understand why their significant other is upset because *her friend* got dumped, but at least they're honest. In fact, in all matters, the ENTP is upfront about their lack of emotional intelligence, and this can make disagreements easier because their partner at least knows why the ENTP is so confused. Communication is key in any relationship, and ENTPs have that covered.

At Work: If there was ever a place that the ENTP's communication skills could shine, it's in the workplace, where they concisely and clearly keep everyone up-to-date on their progress or opinions, refusing to mince words and speaking with a shocking honesty that more people should adopt. They are even better with clients who appreciate a straight-shooter.

26. Becomes excited over the prospect of a challenge

Positive: Some people face an insurmountable task with failure written all over their faces before taking a single step forward. Not the ENTP, who wonders, "Is there even anything out there that requires me to try?" Intellectually brilliant and full of creativity, when ENTPs do find something that actually presents a challenge, they meet it whole-heartedly, with a glimmer of excitement in their eyes.

Negative: This personality type has a tendency to get really excited about something in a very short period of time, and if it has been described as "impossible," the ENTP thinks, "Only because I haven't tried it yet." They throw themselves passionately and unstoppably into it, but this is part of what makes them so careless of other, perhaps more pertinent, tasks.

In Relationships: Playing games with the ENTP will probably get you nowhere (they have that uncanny knack of seeing through people's guises), but if you're genuinely uninterested, and they are fully into you, watch out – you are the mountain cliff that they have sworn to scale, and you're in for some spikey shoes and ropes. Or the social equivalent, whatever that might be.

At Work: Nothing drives coworkers crazy like watching the ENTP gleefully set to work on something that no one else has been able to solve, and nothing makes the ENTP happier than getting their shot at proving their brilliance to everyone. ENTPs would do well to practice a little humility – everyone knows already that they are good at their job.

27. Skilled at solving problems

Positive: ENTPs might not be the people you go to when you need to figure out why your plumbing is acting up, but when it comes to theoretical or ideas-based problems, they are absolutely the type you turn to. Again, they might not know how to change a tire, but they can figure out the best way to get a tow truck to you in five minutes flat.

Negative: The thing about ENTPs and their superior problem-solving skills is that they know they're good at it and they assume that everyone welcomes their advice. Obviously, this is not the case, and ENTPs have a tendency to stick their noses in business that isn't theirs, blissfully ignorant of their unwelcome presence.

In Relationships: ENTPs might furrow their brows as they realize how little they understand about the emotions and feelings of others, but to their credit, when they care about someone they will do whatever they can to hold onto them. This includes turning their open-mindedness and problem-solving skills to the relationship and the issues at hand.

At Work: Obviously in the workplace the ENTP's excellent problem-solving skills can be essential to the work they do, whether it's figuring out how to solve an interpersonal issue or working with a client to discover why exactly they were unhappy with another company's effort (and how they can do better).

28. Sees the possibilities in the world around them

Positive: ENTPs are ideas folks, and it takes next to nothing for them to find inspiration that charges them with whole-hearted enthusiasm. Just by looking around themselves, ENTPs can see the possibilities that are lurking under the surface, whether it's a piece of furniture that can be repurposed or a computer program that is all right, but could be so much better.

Negative: Unfortunately, even though ENTPs are full of ideas for how to improve the world around them, and they are able to see the promise that no one else can, their ideas tend to stop where they start – in their heads – because this personality type lacks the sensing and judging functions which propel thoughts into action.

In Relationships: Despite introverts having the reputation for observing, ENTPs are nonetheless quite perceptive, and that quiet person standing the corner at a party, the one who isn't talking to anyone, enters onto the ENTP radar just the same as the outgoing ENFP who is making everyone laugh. ENTPs won't miss an opportunity to date someone because they overlooked the person.

At Work: ENTPs are exceptionally good brainstormers, especially when they have other people around off of whom they can bounce ideas or even partake in a lively debate over the merits of one idea or another. If you want to push your company in an entire new direction or just freshen up the brand, ask the ENTP for his or her opinion.

29. Might not finish everything they start

Positive: Not every project is a good one; sometimes, we realize halfway in that it's kind of futile and pointless, and to continue would be a waste of time, energy and resources. That's where the ENTP's lack of regret when it comes to not finishing things is a good trait; whereas so many of us would cling to the idea that there will be pay-off (and there isn't), ENTPs cut and run.

Negative: ENTPs don't always distinguish between different kinds of projects, though, so perfectly viable ones can be left in the dust because the ENTP just wasn't excited about it anymore. That's really no reason to quit – imagine if everyone operated along those lines! We'd still be living in caves and hunting for our food.

In Relationships: One of the reasons ENTPs don't finish what they start is because they are better suited to coming up with ideas, rather than actually doing the hands-on work involved. So when the ENTP's partner comes home and finds that her boyfriend left his new desk half-assembled...at least he tried. And then she finishes it while he talks about the latest idea he had for computer software.

At Work: It is incredibly important that ENTPs practice some discipline in the work arena when it comes to finishing projects. At home or with friends, they can get away with it, but leaving work undone will gain them a pretty terrible reputation, and they will soon find that they have no income at all.

30. Makes decisions using reason and logic

Positive: ENTPs can be proud of the fact that they do tend to make good decisions, because they are well-reasoned and thoughtful, even if they aren't thinking that long. In fact, ENTPs are masters of the quick and correct assessment, which is well and good since they tend to be spontaneous.

Negative: As all thinking types are, ENTPs are hopelessly befuddled when it comes to matters of the heart, and they might even try to force their intimidating logic onto emotional situations (to no avail). Sometimes, ENTPs need to let their brains take a break and listen to their guts.

In Relationships: ENTPs need to find a balance between making decisions based on logic – which is the side to which their personalities deeply swing – and choosing to listen to their hearts. With the right feeling partner, they can learn how to identify emotions, both in themselves and others, and yet approach feelings in a well-reasoned way.

At Work: ENTPs are excellent in math and the sciences, specifically theoretical sciences like physics, as well as IT and computer-related fields. If ever there were positions where the application of logic and reason – and perhaps a little intuitive – was key, these would be the areas, and ENTPs should fill the jobs.

31. Self-driven visionaries

Positive: As mentioned, ENTPs only have to look around themselves to feel enthused and inspired. A broken subway system on their way to work or a passing comment by someone in a coffee shop is all the pique the ENTP needs before he or she falls headlong into a thought process that could end up with the development of something new and wonderful.

Negative: Unlike more determined personality types, ENTPs have to work on finding the impetus within themselves to see projects through. While they are excellent self-starters who dream big and for the future, ENTPs have a troubling lack of sensing practicality, as well as the typical perceiving focus difficulties, so they can lose interest before passing the torch onto someone else.

In Relationships: ENTPs aren't just charming and charismatic; their ability to dream big is very attractive to many people. Anyone would be proud to bring home to mom "the woman who invented the latest, hottest social media app" or "the guy who is responsible for the safety features in every car on the road." There is a certain pride attached to dating someone who is capable of making such a huge impact on the world.

At Work: ENTPs don't need bosses cracking the whip at their backs; they are plenty motivated on their own, thank you very much, provided there is some sort of inspiration for them to follow. Even if this personality type does need to collaborate with someone more hands-on, their ability to come up with ideas and push for recognition of them is admirable.

32. At ease in conversations with everyone

Positive: There are a lot of people who go through life looking down and not making eye contact, praying that someone doesn't stop them and try to make them chit-chat. ENTPs are not this type, not in the slightest. They love talking to new people, discovering new points of views that they might not have thought of before and even enjoying some playful banter back and forth.

Negative: Because it doesn't take much for the ENTP to open up and show their true selves in conversation, they can immediately and overwhelmingly cross boundaries that more reserved people would never step over. They just can't help themselves – saying the wild or audacious or even rude, alienating things is who they are.

In Relationships: ENTPs usually get to pick who they want to date, because their ease of conversation makes them accessible and likeable to so many. How they choose from a pool of possible candidates has to do with chemistry, that spark of attraction – surprising for such a logical personality type.

At Work: ENTPs can be thrown into hostile working dinner situations and get everyone chuckling and having a good time (their willingness to pick up the bar tab doesn't hurt, either). If you want to both charm and disarm a tough client who is difficult to please, send in your ENTP, dressed to the nines and primed to persuade.

33. Does not factor others' feelings into decision-making

Positive: Thinking of others is a good thing, but it is not the only thing, and people are prone to consider the feelings of other people when making decisions, when they should actually be considering the most logical option. ENTPs are less likely to be pulled into the emotional woes of others and is capable of making solid, composed decisions.

Negative: Unfortunately, the ENTP will pull out in front of another car because he or she does not care if the person driving it ends up furious or horrified. The ENTP has somewhere they need to be, and they thought that was the fastest way to get there. This personality type can definitely come across as rude and uncaring.

In Relationships: It takes a very strong person to stand up to the ENTP and say, "I'm a part of this relationship, and my opinion matters." But, if anything, the ENTP will respect their partner all the more for doing so, so if you are married to an ENTP and they want to move your family across the country for a job, dig your heels in and tell them they don't get to make the choices without consulting you.

At Work: ENTPs are less prone to be in positions of power or authority, because great responsibility – more than they'd like to be a part of – comes with it. But those who do find themselves climbing the ladder to the top should stop and think about what they say before they say it. Yes, it's good to be honest, but no, making coworkers or subordinates cry on a daily basis is not okay.

www.ingramcontent.com/pod-product-compliance
Lightning Source LLC
Chambersburg PA
CBHW070505290526
45790CB00003B/1104